BETRAYAL OF THE STREETS

Betrayal of the Streets

Danette King

Copyright © 2015 by Danette King.

All rights reserved. No part of this book may be reproduced or transmitted in any form or by any means, electronic or mechanical, including photocopying, recording, or by any information storage and retrieval system, without permission in writing from the copyright owner.

Titles by Danette King

- The Bruises from My Mother's Love

- Betrayal of the Streets

License Statement

This book is licensed for your personal enlightenment and enjoyment.

If you would like to share this book with another person, please purchase an additional copy for each reader.

Author Information
Follow me on twitter @MrsKing
www.danetteking.com
danetteking@youngcreativeminds.com

About the Author

Danette King has been a fighter all of her life. Born July 30, 1974 in Chicago, IL, she has faced and overcame many adversities including coming from a broken family and having to enter the judicial system at an early age. Danette is a proud parent of seven children. Losing her second child to death at the age of 16 and suffering from multiple forms of abuse. She has dedicated her life to changing the lives and views of the youth of today.

She has done multiple services and given countless donations to the Austin Township Community and has worked for other community organizations to help establish a healthier living environment for today's urban youth. Through her love and passion for children and impoverished teens, she founded Young Creative Minds Youth Organization (2007) -which has etched quite a reputation within itself. She created and facilitated the infamous West-Side Beat the Street Spelling Bee (created within the Austin Community, this event was catered to Chicago Public School District to promote literacy awareness and good sportsmanship among peers as well as scholastic acceleration), YCM Landscaping Services (teenagers that were either on probation or parole had the option to complete their community service through this program and also had a later opportunity to be employed for their services), and the Community Salute Concert Series (finding yet another innovative way to give back to her community, she orchestrated a free concert for underprivileged children who couldn't afford concert tickets to see their favorite artists), just to name a few of her many attributes to her community. Danette uses her past pains as her strengths in order to pave a road for children and young adults that have or are currently traveling a path that she has once traveled.

From speaking of past pains from abusive and non-cohesive relationships to dealing one on one with Chicago's underground drug cartel, she continues to inspire young women as well as young men to be more than what the system has stereotyped them: a statistic. These endeavors good and bad had led Danette to become an "author" ready to share her testimony to the world. Danette claimed the profession "author" in 2010 and released her first book in March 2012, The Bruises from my Mother's Love, a seven book series that is taking the world by storm. Danette has also received multiple accolades from city alderman and even mayor Daley himself, and as long as she continues to be a standing pillar in the urban community, she is sure to receive much more in the future.

Dedication

This is the second book of my seven book series and it is dedicated to those that went through physical, mental, sexual, and emotional abuse. My series will also be a blessing to those that are the abusers, giving them a clear and precise understanding of what goes on in the mind of the ones they hurt and maybe someday apologize to give them closure. It's never too late to take back your life.

"Open the window to your heart and free all of your pain."

Matthew 18:21, 22 Peter came to Jesus and asked, "Lord, how many times shall I forgive my brother when he sins against me? Up to seven times?" Jesus answered, "I tell you, not seven times, but seventy-seven times. (Followed by the parable of the ungrateful servant).......35 "This is how my heavenly Father will treat each of you unless you forgive your brother from your heart."

Author Danette King

Acknowledgments

There are many people in my life that inspire me and support my dreams; however I have a few that put in overtime just to see me smile. These are the people that supported me even when I didn't believe in myself, their inspiring words and support helped me to be productive and stay proactive. I want to show endless love to God to whom is the head of my life, my children the ones that never stop loving me inspite of my short comings Tieshia, Jeffrey, Jamarr, Jessica, Terrell, Otis, and Keyshawn, my grandchildren Adrian, Matthew and Madison, my sisters Deidre and Danyell, my brothers DeAndre and Raynard, my best friends Ed Akeel, Antionette Brown, Angela Jennings, Tony Hampton, Myron Vance , and Zanovia Blackmon, my publicist April Adams, much love to my editor Beverly Bradley whom was also my English instructor in college, much love to A'Tiffany Michas being the very first to read my first book also I wanted to show love to a very special young lady that have cheered me on since the first day she met me Kentoria Hampton. Last but not least much love to my family on my father side the Barnes and McCullum family, and special thanks to my uncle Richard Barnes for believing in me and speaking encouraging words into me when I just wanted to give up.

Introduction

Well it's me, Lunye', just as I promised, I'm back with Book Two of my seven book Memoir series.

This book will **not** only have you on the edge of your seats, but you will think twice before trusting people you just meet on the streets.

As I told you before, life wasn't a walk in the park with my mother, growing up. The way she treated me led me to the only place I could turn to; yeah, you guessed it, "the streets". My last journey of running away was like a breath of fresh air, although it was quite scary, but in my mind nothing could be scarier than being in the house with my mother.

1

The last time I went out for one of my getaways, I got locked out the house and I figured taking a chance on knocking on the door to get back in was too risky, I would rather have a fist fight with an angry ape than knock on that door and wake up my mother, so I just went back on the block to see if there was anyone else still outside, just as I thought, everyone was gone in, so I just sat in the park thinking about the awesome time I had with Devin.

I began reminiscing about our talk and how fine he was, he had me feeling kind of strange, but a good strange. Oh! Let me tell you, he had the sexiest smile I ever seen, his teeth were as white as the outside of an egg shell. He was about 5'8", dark mocha colored skin that glistened in the dark, his hair was wavy and short, he always wore the nicest clothing and the up-to-date gym shoes. He just made me feel warm inside.

Then I my thoughts were interrupted by this guy, LaSalle. He was walking down the street rapping, and I must say he sounded horrible.

However, I was glad to see somebody because it was dark and I was really scared. I was pretty cool with LaSalle even though he was a pervert.

"What are you doing out so late?" he asked.

First, I tried to act as if my mother was cool as ever and just allowed me to go out whenever I wanted too, not even giving it a second thought to what I said, the words just rolled off my tongue, that's when I realized I just sounded dumb as ever.

He replied, "Girl you must think I'm slow or stupid or something?"

Well in the back of my mind I really did think he was "stupid or something", little did he know. I just stood there in total silence, searching my mind for a rebuttal, but somehow my brain bank was out of service.

LaSalle had this look on his face as if he was ready to slap the shit out of me, but he just said "I know damn well your momma ain't letting your young ass hang out this late".

I felt as if he uncovered my whole top secret operation and I just dropped my head with shame, but laughing in the inside at the same time.

"You just think you know everything", I couldn't think of anything else to say so I said a common but safe response.

"Why are you outside so late? I know your momma be tripping about you being out late too", I then asked him, but in the back of my mind I was thinking if he was my child I wouldn't give a damn either, only because he was a jerk.

"Hell yeah, she be tripping, but she in the crib sleep." He said.

I said, "Well since you want to be so damn nosey, I had been sneaking out the crib so I can just breathe a little bit. I was going back in the crib, but when I tried to go back in to my surprise the door was locked. So I took it upon myself to just stay out because I didn't want to get my ass fried for trying to come out, and kick it."

He looked at me and just shook his head. "Your momma gonna whip your ass so bad you gonna need an engineer to put it back together again".

"Look you making my damn stomach hurt, boy!" I just said.

I felt like I had to shit, "Stop cracking jokes about it, you gonna make me shit on myself."

What he didn't know was, I had been farting the whole time I been talking to him because I was nervous as hell.

I got straight to the point and asked him if it was okay for me to stay over at his house because I didn't have anywhere else to go.

He said, "you gonna mess around and make me get my ass whipped too girl, but since you my girl and I would really feel bad if something happened to you out here and besides I got mad love for you, it's cool as long as my mother don't catch you."

I was cool with that as long as I didn't have to go home, anything was better than home at that point especially considering what my mother had in store for me.

Quiet as kept I really needed a vacation away from the beatings anyway.

We made our way to his house and he made it clear that I had to sleep under the bed and I told him I was fine with that even though in the back of my mind I wasn't too happy about laying on the damn hard ass floor but hey, beggars can't be choosey in this life.

But one thing I can say is that he made sure he brought me food and made sure I had covers and pillows to keep me comfortable and warm.

Although he was feeding me and trying to make me feel comfortable, he had his own agenda behind his kind actions. In his little sick mind he wanted some butt for his kind services but I had a rude awaking waiting for his raggedy ass.

While he was plotting in that small brain of his, I was creating a master plan of my own. I just sat waiting on him to make his move.

He had the nerve to ask me if he can come chill with me under the bed and that's when that weird feeling came about, you know the turning of the stomach and the sudden sweaty palms. That is what I call a sudden outbreak of pervert alert, little nasty bastard.

At first I tried to play it off and giggle my way out of it, "Boy please stop playing with me! It's not enough room under here for both of us and furthermore, what if your mother walked in and noticed that you were not in the bed?"

He replied she hardly ever come in his room at night and I said if she hardly come why did you say I had to sleep under the bed? He gave me a phony chuckle saying I just want to be on the safe side and I said yeah right.

So, that kinda kept him tamed for a while. We started watching TV and in my mind I was in safe mode, but I still had my antenna on alert. I began to think he wasn't a bad dude because he didn't try to make a move for a while.

I began to get sleepy and comfortable, I was so tired before I knew it I nodded off and before I could even close my eyes good this nappy head bastard was under the bed, touching my breast.

This pissed me off 'cause when I woke up I thought I was at home and my stepfather was on the prowl again. But reality kicked in and just as I thought, it was this musty animal face demon. At this point I felt kinda relieved because I could handle his nasty ass.

I had to put this premature rapist in his place so I bent his fingers backwards and smacked his face. I told him to get his hands off me and then this demon had the nerve to get mad and told me to shut up before his mama heard me.

"You wouldn't have to worry about your mother hearing me if you keep your damn hands to yourself."

I guess I pissed him off and he told me I had to leave. I was about to get up and leave until my light bulb lit up in my head, this trick don't even supposed to be having company in the first place.

I told him I wasn't going no damn where. He looked at me as if he was shocked and defeated.

I said, "You ain't never about send me outside at two o'clock in the morning by myself."

He said, "Well that don't got shit to do with me"

I said, "If I have to go then I'm going to wake your mother up and tell on your little nasty ass and we both gonna be ass out."

Now I had his attention and he knew I meant business. Even though he was mad he knew that I was very serious. I felt like if I got be on the streets at two o'clock in the morning then you gonna get your ass whipped two o'clock in the morning.

I know it sounded evil but he had me messed up. I finally went to sleep and trust me I slept like a bear, before you knew, it was eight in the morning. He woke me up and said, "You go have to hurry up and leave before my momma get up."

I was cool with that, so I got up stretching as if I didn't have a worry in the world.

As I was putting on my shoes I had the nerve to ask him if he had some cereal, he told me no, but I knew he was lying, I didn't say anything cause I had made him suffer enough.

He opened his room door and peeked out, he looked back at me and told me to come on before she get up, and me being an ass, I took my sweet time.

As soon as I walked out, he slammed the door so fast he damn near caught the hairs on the back my neck. When I got outside, the sun was glaring in my eyes, it was irritating me, and so I put my hands over my eyes to block the sun from blinding me. I didn't have a clue where I was going, I just let my legs lead the way.

As I was walking, my stomach began to growl like a lion in the wilderness with no signs of prey. Now what was I going to eat? I had no money and I had no other alternatives, being new to the streets begging was not an option because my pride would not let me, so I walked to the neighborhood grocery store and went to the fruit department and it was like I had my own buffet.

It was kind of embarrassing to just go and just start grabbing fruit and just start maxing as if I owned the store. I finally got the nerve to walk over by the fruit and start moving the fruit around as if I was about to buy some. Then I gradually moved over by the grapes, grabbed one and looked around to see if I had an audience.

When I had seen that the coast was clear I helped myself. Those grapes was so damn good I just wanted to find the store manager and let him know that the fruit was on point.

But we know that I had to lay low 'cause I was doing something I had no business doing. Okay, even though I had no money and I was in there having my way filling my belly with sweet, delicious fruit. I didn't want to get too comfortable so I walked myself over to the candy aisle.

Thank God for Brach's candy because the layout was wonderful, it was so many different candies from cherry slices to caramel candy. I felt like I was in heaven, I almost forgot that what I was doing was illegal. As I was indulging myself in the candy reality kicked in and it wasn't pretty, when someone tapped me on my shoulder, it was one of the workers staring me down as if it was judgment day.

I immediately began to gravitate my weight to assume the running position because going to jail for eating candy was not an option at the time and because I had other things on my agenda like "being free!"

Before I could run the lady said, "Baby if you hungry I can give you a couple of dollars to get you something to eat."

I didn't know if I should take the money or run, but it seemed like a good idea for me to just to take the money and say thank you and go on about my business. So I took the money, although I was hesitant, and told her that I was sorry and said thank you.

She told me before I left, to make this the last time that I came in there stealing. I told her you don't have to worry. But in my mind I had a whole different conversation, telling myself how stupid I was for getting caught and how the next time I would do things a lot different.

I finally walked off feeling so shame, I turned back around to look and see if she was still watching me and sure as sweaty ass stank she stood there until I walked out the door.

Now I was outside in front of the store, I almost felt home free because for some reason I just knew she was go send security after me. My heart pace speeded up as I got closer to the sidewalk of freedom and I didn't dare to look back because I didn't want to see security run up on me.

As I took that last step to sweet freedom, the smile of success was written all over my face, it was if I got away with stealing some expensive jewels. When I finally made it around the corner I opened my hands and counted the money the nice lady gave me. Although the money was sweaty because of my hands where sweating like Eskimo in a sauna fully dressed, to my surprise I counted up like eight dollars and forty cents. I had like a million and one thoughts going through my head at that time, like what I was going to buy to eat and where would I go to rest and watch T.V.

I began walking again and I walked for at least 15 minutes before my nose began to smell a smell that I recognized yes, Lawd Mickey D's!

I wanted to run and just bust down doors and order everything on the menu, but reality kicked back in and of course those eight dollars could only go so far. So as I walked in to the castle of the Big Mac, my stomach began to let off a ferocious growls and I immediately stepped in line to order my food.

As I stood in line, I believe I studied that menu as if I was studying for a major test for school. I finally got to the front of the line and the cashier finally said the magic words

"Can I take your order?"

I stood there first in shock because this was something I have wished for because I don't remember eating Mickey D's to often at home,

The cashier asked me again "Can I take your order?"

"Can I have the Big Mac meal, please?" I finally responded.

She replied, "Sure that will be $3.99"

I was happy because that meant I had change left to buy some other things.

I waited on my food and paced back and forth until that magical moment finally came. The bag of happiness! All I could do is smile and grab a seat. I couldn't demolish this meal without thanking the almighty God, because, who knows when the next time I will eat from Mickey D's?

When I took the first bite from the Big Mac I felt like I was in heaven, and I could only just continue to indulge myself and eat. Fifteen minutes later the food was gone, and I only wished I could have rewound that moment a thousand times. I made sure I took a trip to the bathroom before I left so I could release my bowels and freshen up before getting back to my journey.

As I left Mickey D's, I felt like a queen, I had no worries for that moment until I realized that I was back walking with no place to go, but I had a full stomach and I had a few bucks left in my pockets, I was planning on holding on to that until later.

For some odd reason I begin to talk to an unseen person, I didn't have a clue to who I was talking to and the craziest part about it, I couldn't see him or her. I began to just talk as if whomever it was talking back to me. I was just wanted someone to talk to at the time and that person was the only person at that time who would listen. I began to cry and just ask that person to help me because I was tired; I even asked myself who was I talking too?

I knew very little about God at the time but what I've seen and that's only when people sat down and ate and they would thank him for food. I ask myself today was my spirit drawn to God, even though I didn't really know who he was.

But nonetheless, whoever I was speaking to always made me feel better afterwards. I had to quickly get myself back in survival mode because a crying girl my age on the streets of Chicago was very dangerous. So, there I was back on my journey.

2

I was on my way to nowhere and I decided to go over a guy's house that I went to school with, his name was Renzo.

Now Renzo was a guy that I had a crush on in school and he would always put a smile on my face and he would always be there to protect me when someone would bother me, in school, he gave me a sense of security.

Renzo was also a handsome boy, he had dark skin and it was so smooth, he was also kind of buff and just a tad bit taller than I, he also had the prettiest eyes, they were hazel. Renzo just made me feel good anytime I set eyes on him.

This guy was my knight in shining armor. I went to his house and I was just praying he was home because only God knew where I was going to go next.

The closer I got to the building, my heart began to beat rapidly, reason being I can't explain the reason. As I reached my hand towards the door to the building, I hesitated for a moment because I was nervous, I did a mirror check to make sure I was looking good, now of course I did not have a mirror but I was able to check myself out in the glass of the door.

I walked up the stairs silently so I was able to listen by their door but the noise from the TV drowned out all of the voices.

I knocked on the door.

"Who is it?" he answered

I said Ne-Ne and he opened the door and it was like Fourth of July in my spirit! I always felt kind of warm on the inside whenever I saw him.

When he opened the door I had a timid look on my face and he asked me what made me come over his house and I said I was just out kicking it and he said stop lying 'cause he knew that my mother wouldn't even let me sit on the porch, so how would I just be wandering the neighborhood.

He finally told me to come in and I saw his little brother sitting on the couch watching T.V and it was my favorite show, The Flintstones.

I stood by the door at first and he told me that I could sit down and I was feeling really good at this point because he felt like my savior because he gave me a place to just relax.

I started watching T.V and he asked me if I wanted something to drink or if I was hungry and I said no I'm good because I just got through eating at Mickey D's and he said why you ain't bring me none and I said I didn't even know I was coming over here.

He said, "Girl I was just playing."

I smiled at him as if I was in love, I didn't really know how it felt to be in love but I was sure at that time that I was in love because those feelings I had for him had me on cloud nine. I sat on the couch and watched T.V for about 20 minutes before his mother walked in and I just wanted to run.

When she came through the door she was like an angel. She spoke to me very softly, said hello and I felt a sense of relief and said hello back.

I was so shocked that his mother didn't snap, maybe I thought this was because my mother would have reacted totally different. It would have been like World War II in that house if it was my mother.

Renzo introduced me to his mom and it was like she didn't mind that I was there and I thought to myself this must be my lucky day. I got caught stealing and I didn't go to jail and the lady that caught me gave me some money and then I had Mickey D's and then I was able to hang out with a boy that I had a crush on in school it doesn't get any better than this.

Now I am really in relax mode, she went into her room and I fell asleep about ten minutes later. Before I knew it Renzo was waking me up telling me to go lay in his bed and I asked him if he would get in trouble and he said no his mother was cool and she didn't trip like that, so I went in his room and laid on his bed.

O.M.G! His bed smelled so good and it was so comfortable! He had like three pillows and he had a huge T.V. in his room. I had so many thoughts running through my head at that time, I was just wishing I could be there forever, but I knew that could never happen.

Renzo came in the room and laid down with me, I was feeling kind of weird when he did that but at the same time it felt good. He put his arm around me and I just felt so safe, before I knew it I was sleep.

Time went by so fast and when I woke up it was dark outside and I noticed that he wasn't in the room anymore so I got up and looked around; his mom was in her room and his brother was watching TV.

Renzo was in the kitchen cooking and by the way that kitchen smelled was the aroma of a professional. I told him I was about leave 'cause it was late but in the back of my head I really wanted to stay cause I was extra hungry and I really didn't have anywhere to go. I was just hoping and praying he would just say stay.

To my surprise he said "What you leaving for? I'm in here making you something to eat."

I told him that I didn't really want to be out to late and I had to find me somewhere to stay.

He said, "What you mean you have to find somewhere to stay?"

I told him I ran away from home and he said he would and go ask his mother if I could stay here for a few days, and as I patiently waited, I began to have all sorts of weird feelings; like my stomach was bubbling and my head started to hurt because I just knew his mom was go say hell no!

He went to his mom's room and asked her and she wanted to know why I couldn't go home and he told her that my momma was always beating on me and I had ran away from home and I was waiting on my daddy to come from out of town to get me. In my mind I thought he was slick as ever, but at the same time I loved it because I just wanted to be with him.

Never in a million years did I think his mother was going to say yes but she did and I just smiled at him and he smiled back. So he made chicken and potatoes for the whole house. You can trust and believe his mother raised him well because that boy could cook better than some adults.

I waited patiently for the food to get done although my stomach sounded like a roar of thunder because I was so hungry.

For a moment I was lost in thought, day dreaming, as if I lived with him and we were young adults like maybe 18 or 19 and just looking at him at the stove cooking allowed me to imagine us together in our own place.

As I sat there I had my hand under my chin with a big Kool-Aid smile on my face until I was startled by the door bell ringing. My heart began to race because I was scared that my mother was at the door with a bat ready to beat the oxygen out of me.

He went to the window and yelled out asking who is it? I began to move toward the back door so if it was her I could just take flight.

Oh, what a relief it was his mom's friend OMG! I was so happy, words just couldn't explain how happy I was. Anyway, he informed his mom her friend was at the door and she pretty much blew her off. I was kind of happy she blew her off cause I didn't feel like answering any questions, like who are you? And all the other mess, you know black folks can be nosey at times.

Now I am really excited cause my guy hollered out come and get it those were like the words of the promise land. I sat at the table and I grabbed my fork and started to chow down. They looked at me as if I was an animal.

Renzo said, "We say grace around here."

I was so embarrassed, so I just followed suit.

"God is good God is great, let us thank you for our food. Amen!"

I thought to myself I like this it was short and sweet and on top that you were telling God thank you for providing us with food, so I kind of stored it in my mind to use in the future.

Although I have heard people bless their food before, but I only did it as a solo act, when I was damn near starving, never as a family. We ate and without any questions, I washed the dishes. This was like a systematic thing with me because my mom didn't play that *let my food digest* thing. Soon as you eat, get your ass up and wash those dishes and go to bed. But for some odd reason it didn't feel bad or troublesome here because I was in a calm and peaceful environment.

I washed those dishes with a smile on my face and took my time with no one over my shoulder stressing me. Now the dishes were done and Renzo he fixed the couch up for me because his mother didn't play that sleeping in the same bed overnight if you were not married.

Lights out, shoes off, it was time to rest and sleep. I kind of eased my shoes off because I knew they had a stench to them, I had slept with my shoes on the night before, so I waited 'till he left the living room and when I thought they were sleep I went into the bathroom, washed my feet, washed my socks and washed the insides of my shoes.

I tipped toed back into the living room and laid down, and stared at the ceiling for about maybe thirty minutes until I finally went to sleep smiling and nervous at the same time.

Something woke me up and I believed it was that unseen person again, so I begin to talk to that person telling that person how my day went and how I wish everyday could be this way and I always felt this unseen person always cared about what I had to say. I heard a noise and I hurried and closed my eyes because I didn't want anyone to think that I was crazy and before you knew I was knocked out.

I awoke again, this time to the smell of bacon and fresh coffee coming from the kitchen, the nightmare of me being home dissolved out of my mind for that brief moment. It was Renzo's mom cooking and she looked over at me and said good morning sweetie and I smiled and said good morning back. She asked me if I was hungry and I said no, but that was because I just didn't want to continue to beg and wear out my welcome.

She told me that if I changed my mind it was some left on the stove and I said okay!

Renzo was still sleep and I felt like I was too needy and I thought maybe I was getting on his nerves so I went to the bathroom and washed my face and told his mom to tell him I will be right back, but in the back of my mind I was taking off.

I knew he would be upset but he would get over it. It was early in the morning and I didn't have a clue where I was headed, so I wandered off to the park; it was like about seven o'clock in the morning and I always enjoyed hanging In the park; the sweet sound of nature always kept me calm and I always felt free, I got to talk to my unseen friend whom at the time I may have thought it was my imaginary friend.

As I got closer to the park, my stomach began to growl, but I only had a few dollars left in my pocket and plus nothing was open. I kept going back and forth in my mind because I wanted to go back to Renzo's house where it was nice and safe and quiet and plenty of food. But me and my pride, it always put me in a bad situation.

It was this weird feeling I kept having in my stomach but I just couldn't figure out what it was, you know like the feeling I had when I was at LaSalle's house, the pervert alert and it was so strong, I had sweaty palms and all and I was thinking maybe I should just at least call and tell his mom that I wasn't coming back so I walked until I found a pay phone.

After walking about three blocks, I finally found a pay phone, so I dug in my pocket and found a quarter and put it in the phone and dialed the number and just my luck the phone took my money, so I beat on the phone for like a minute or so, then I went to check my pockets for another quarter and I came up empty.

I guess it wasn't meant for me to call or something so I just start walking toward the park again. The same weird feeling came back again and I just kind of blew it off because it was quite annoying and plus I was thinking about how worried Renzo was going to be once he figured out I wasn't coming back.

I finally made it to the park there was the sound of sweet success the birds chirping the trees withering the smell of the grass freshly cut.

I entered the park and began to walk on the trail, I was extra tired so I sat on the bench to rest because I was still tired and for some reason that weird feeling came back again and would not go away.

My attention focused on this strange station wagon. It was like four men in there and they were eating Mickey D's. I knew that because I saw the wrappers they threw from the car and furthermore I have a nose like a blood hound.

The driver was staring at me so I got up and walked over to another bench where they couldn't see me.

Now I felt a little better and just needed to rest just for a while. There I was in the park relaxing and the sound of the birds and the trees withering and the fresh smell of fresh cut grass relax me so I nodded off.

3

The sound of a loud thump awoke me, I thought maybe I fell off the bench or something. When I opened my eyes and I wasn't able to see clearly, I saw images that resembled two men in front of me and I was in total shock. I thought to myself maybe it's time for me to wake up from this nightmare, but I felt something leaking on my neck so I knew at this point whatever was going on was a reality, I grasped the back of my head and it was bleeding. I tried to get up and run, take off, but what I didn't know it was somebody behind me and he was one of the guys that I saw in the station wagon and the other guys were in front of me too.

At this point, I just knew my life was flashing right before me, but that dull thumping pain reminded me that I needed to escape before they kill me. So, I tried to scream and one of the guys put his hands around my mouth.

They dragged me over to the bushes. It was like ten bushes over where they took me and I was so scared and confused. One of the guys pulled out his penis and told me to suck it or he was going to cut my throat and I couldn't believe this was happening. My heart begins to pound like an elephant stomping in a parade and didn't understand why this was happening to me. In the back of my mind I was hoping this was a dream and I would wake up any minute. In such a short time I had all these different emotions invading my mind all at once.

Before I could plea for my freedom all I know it was lights out for me cause I couldn't tell you what happen after that, but I do remember the scent of several different cologne's and the smell of blood and dirt.

I woke up with someone over me asking if I was dead and for a minute I thought I was because I couldn't feel my body and I noticed my clothes had been taken off and were missing. I was hoping I had an awful nightmare, but reality kicked in when I tried to get up and move it felt like I have been ran over by a semi-truck, my body felt so heavy and numb at the same time.

Then I remembered this guy saying just lay still because you are bleeding pretty bad and then I remembered looking down by my legs, it was blood all over my thighs and I smelled blood in the air so I began to panic, I could feel my heart racing so fast that it made me think that I was about to die.

But on another note, I was more focused on getting up and fleeing from the scene than going to the hospital, because I knew that the police would start asking questions and they would find out that I was a runaway and they would mean I had to go back home to my mom.

So by the time I gathered my strength to raise my body up, the sound of the fire truck startled me. At this point, I just knew that my adventure was over when the fire truck pulled up I just laid back down and looked puzzled, thinking to myself why would the fire truck be here and I also was thinking of a phony name to come up with so I lifted my head up as the fireman walked over and asked me to lay back down, sweetheart and I really didn't want to, I really wanted to run until I realized that I couldn't go far because I was naked.

I remember I didn't have any clothes on, OMG! This has brought forward a whole new emotion, yep, you guessed, it humiliation. I was put on a gurney and put into the ambulance, from that point on all I could hear is the lady paramedic asking me all kinds of questions and at the same time the irritating sound of those damn sirens.

I remember the ambulance moving really fast and I began to think about the time when my mother caught me outside playing without permission and she just started beating my ass right outside where I was hanging out and when I tried to get up and run she kicked me in my back so hard I slid on the concrete and all I could feel my skin separating from my body and my dress going up in the air showing off my panties, as I got up I could feel the blood leaking from my legs, but I was too scared to look down, all I could do is look in the back of me and make sure I got to the house ASAP.

My thoughts were quickly interrupted because of the bumpy driveway leading to the hospital. The ambulance doors opened and there the other paramedic was waiting to pull the gurney out.

The paramedics began pushing me into the hospital, I heard the doors open and I remember the lights were really bright and I remembered a nurse asking me if I could tell them what happened and I remembered not saying anything and she kept trying to ask more questions and I kept ignoring her so she left and another lady came in, but this time it wasn't a nurse, it was a lady with some nice clothes on and she also wanted to ask more questions, just as I ignored the nurse, I ignored her too.

Then about ten minutes later the police came in, one male cop and one female cop and began to ask me questions, like what was my name and where did I live and how old was I, but I knew if I told them the truth I would be headed back to my mother's hell hole.

So at this point I was nervous and confused and I knew if I didn't say something they were going to start snooping and they were going to find out, so I blurted out a phony name, Tonya Hill and I lied about my age and said I was eighteen years old. They asked for contact info for my parents and of course I lied and said they were deceased and they asked for any next of kin and I told them that they were in Mississippi.

In my mind, I thought I may have fooled them, but they just knew I was lying. So when the officers approached me again they told me if I didn't tell the truth that I was going be in a lot of trouble.

So I stuck to the same story until they left. The other lady, with the nice clothes, came in again and now I knew she was a rape advocate and she was so nice to I couldn't resist telling her what had happened. She called in the officers and I confirmed my story with them. The doctor and nurse started what they called a rape kit, which I really wasn't ready for it, but I had to get it over with; the doctor was so nice and for some reason he kept saying it wasn't my fault, which I knew, but I kept saying to myself if I hadn't ran away I wouldn't be in this situation.

After all the chitter-chatter with them it was time for me to make my move to sneak out, but I couldn't go anywhere without clothes, so I waited around so I could find some to steal. But to my surprise, the police were back and asking more questions.

They were asking me if I could describe the guys and I described them to the best of my ability. The police asked me if I remembered anything specific about them or about the vehicle they were in and as I began to think back I remembered three letters of the license plate. I blurted out "GYC" and I saw the officer taking notes as I was talking. The nurse came in and gave me some jogging pants and a sweat shirt. This was exactly what doctor ordered because I wanted to make my move soon.

The officers were beginning to make me feel uneasy because of the questioning, I felt as if they were trying to make me re-live the rape over and over in my head when all I wanted to do was to forget.

The officers finally left the room and they instructed me to stay in the room and they would come back shortly, but in the back of my mind I had other plans, like escaping and leaving it all behind me as if it didn't happen. I than began to cry, I remember wanting to die. I felt as if my life was over. I didn't understand why I was even born because from the time I can remember my life was a living hell.

My heart raced with anticipation and a little voice in the back of my mind kept telling me to not leave, but I weighed my options and I figured they were going to send me back home to my mother and at that point I felt fleeing would be a better option because I knew in my heart that my mother wasn't going to give me a welcome home party after running away.

I had about a million thoughts racing through my mind within ten seconds. Once I snapped out of my trance, I then made the decision to run for it.

I jumped off the bed, my body felt like it had been badly beaten, but the physical damage was nothing compared to the emotional damage that was inflicted on me. I walked toward the door and it open just enough so I could peek out and observe the hallway, there was a lot of movement and chatter out there, but there was no signs of the officers, so I eased my way out of the room and frantically walked toward the sign that said Exit and without looking back.

I felt as if I had been walking for about fifteen minutes, but in actuality I was only walking for about fifteen seconds. Finally I saw another exit sign and I began to pick up the pace, my heart was beating so fast and loud I thought I was having a heart attack. I told myself not to look back, but I couldn't help but to look back and thank God the coast was clear.

I was free again, but mentally I was locked away. It's sad to say after all the trauma; I would rather run back to the streets than go home. However, it might sound stupid, but for me it made plenty of sense.

Ok, so now I am free, what was my next move? I didn't have a clue so I just began on walking. There I was walking and walking and then I walked some more, I began to feel the need to talk to my unseen friend.

I remember asking my friend why can't I have a normal life like other kids and I could have sworn my friend said because I was special, and that made me smile for a moment, but I still didn't understand why was life so hard for me.

I began to just cry and I took a seat on a stoop of someone's porch. I didn't have a clue whose porch I was sitting on, but I needed to rest and think. I always asked myself and my unseen friend why I had to be born and I could help it but my eyes would tear up even more.

I cried so hard that my breath was short. At that point I just leaned back on the concrete wall that was connected to the stoop and began to look up at the sky and for at that moment I began to feel at peace with just the movement of the clouds. I began to think about the rape and think about what I could have did to prevent it from happening. I thought momentarily about just killing myself and it would just end all of my misery. I even thought of ways that I could kill myself but the things I thought about would be very painful so that wasn't an option at that particular time.

The loud sound of some kids my age interrupted my peace time. They were coming out of the door next to the building I was in front of, so I got up and began to walk again.

While I was walking, my thoughts began to race again and I then began to get dizzy and began to panic. I had to take control of myself and get it together because I knew that I had to focus on where I would rest and my next meal.

The more I walked the more I noticed that my damn feet were killing me the shoes I had on my feet were hurting like hell. My feet felt like someone was crushing my dam pinky toe with a nut cracker.

However, I kept my pain camouflaged so that no one would notice, but when I was alone I slid those jelly bean sandals off and allowed my toes to expand to their true size. I realized that the pain I was experiencing was nothing compared to the pain that I was experiencing mentally.

4

Back to my original thoughts!

In my mind I thought I was free, but I really created another prison that would someday cause serious mental pain. Although I been raped and my body felt violated, I continued on with my journey, to where? I didn't have a clue.

I walked and I walked, before I knew it hours passed and I became very tired and hungry so I had to think quickly of a master plan and not even a couple of seconds later a light bulb popped up over my head. I always think better under pressure.

I went over to a girl's house who I barely knew, but I knew her enough to cop a squat at her house for the night because her mom was a crack head and she wouldn't even noticed if I stayed the night or not.

The only thing that made me feel uneasy about going to her place is because a lot of men would be over there and the house was filthy. At this point I couldn't be choosey because I damn sure wasn't going back home. I made it to the block of Erie and something in the inside of me kept yelling for me to turn around, but my legs kept walking forward. I made it four houses away from her house and before you know it I could smell the stench of piss already, but I kept walking towards her house anyway. I made it to the front porch and I noticed one of the steps were broken after I damn near broke my ankle on it.

I could hear the loud chatter in the house before I got to the door. O.M.G I was so hesitant on knocking on that door but I just went ahead and knocked anyway. I heard a loud voice yell "COME IN" In my mind, I thought wow! Do people ask who is it anymore? Hmmmm!

Despite my thoughts I walked in and look around and for a brief second the inside of the house had so much smoke and so many people in there I began to panic and in that short time my heart began to beat rapidly and the room began to spin very fast and I began to get very dizzy and I started to feel like I wanted to throw up and scream all at the same time, but a loud voice made me snap out of it "Who are you looking for?"

I stood there in shock because it was the voice of a man and the voice was so deep it vibrated through my bones. He asked a second time and I answered Shonda.

Shonda is someone I met through another friend I knew from my old neighborhood, so the guy that answered the door screamed out Shonda's name and said that somebody was at the door for her and at that point I was so relieved that she was there because I didn't have a clue to what where I was going to go.

Shonda came to the door and at first she was like who are you looking for and I thought in the back of my head like damn, she don't even remember me, so I said quickly that this is me, Na Na and said Tasha was a friend.

She said "What Tasha?"
"

"From off Chicago Ave."
"Oh. Tasha ain't over here."
"I knew that."
"What's up then?"

And I told her that I needed somewhere to chill at because the police was looking for me and to my surprise she told me to come on up without asking anything else.

I felt at this point this was just too sweet, so I began to babble and she seemed to not really care, so I just did what I did best, just shut up, went in and followed her to her room. In the back of my mind I wanted tell her what I went through earlier, but for some reason I didn't feel right talking about it, so I walked her room, it was pretty tidy in there, but I couldn't say the same for the rest of the house.

Shonda flopped down on her bed and told me that I could have a seat and she grabbed the house phone and started talking as if prior to me coming over she was talking to someone. I sat down thinking, what if she call Tasha and tell her I came over her house begging for a place to stay? Or even worst call the police.

As I sat down, I was listening to her conversation with whoever and it seemed to me she was talking to a boy. I just made myself at home and kind of just fell into chill mode until I heard a loud noise like someone was fighting, so Shonda said to whoever she was talking to let her call them back and I began to panic.

She ran out of the room and I was looking for an exit route in her room, I walked over to the window and it was sealed shut, so I really start panicking. She came back in the room and told me, "Girl come on because my brother and my uncle are fighting again and I don't have time for this bullshit."

I began to follow her to the front door and I had no idea where we were going. As we finally got close to the front door, her brother and uncle came tumbling towards us and my reaction was so embarrassing; I just blurted out the loudest scream. At that moment was like everything just froze and everyone was looking at me. Within that ten seconds I was trying think of an excuse why I would scream like that and I just said "Y'all bumped into me and hurt my leg!"

Well that's the best I could come up with at the time.

"What the hell y'all looking at her like that? Shit y'all scared the hell out her!" The lady looked really sick who said that, and her clothing wasn't positioned on her right, I didn't care that she came to my rescue.

I realized it was Shonda's mom because she said, "Shonda y'all can go back to the room cause these motherfuckers are about to get the hell out of here with the bullshit."

I then began to calm down because I was so riled up on the inside I could have very well had had a heart attack and not even know it.

Shonda said, "Okay Ma!"

So, we went back to Shonda's room and she began to fuss and say how tired she was of this house and everyone in it. I just looked puzzled and had nothing to reply back with.

Immediately she changed the subject and said, "So when was the last time you talked to Tasha?"

"About a couple of weeks ago." But in the back of my mind I was so glad to be off the conversation of her dysfunctional family problems.

Shonda said, "Girl you know we got into it."

With relief again in the back of my head I said thank you God.

I replied "Naw girl I haven't seen her in a long time."

Then she began to tell me what went down and I really didn't care because this worked out in my favor. I listened, but at the same time I was thinking about the rape and how I was going to deal with this for the rest of my life.

Suddenly while I was having my own thoughts, I remembered she said something about a fight and she immediately got my attention. I replied what fight, so she could repeat what she said.

She said, "Girl, I just can't believe this girl tried to front me off in front of some boys and smacked me and I just rushed her ass and beat the hell out of her."

I was so happy in the inside because that meant there will be no communication between the two.

So, back to her conversation, I began to act like I was so surprised and then I told her that Tasha was selfish and she was no good anyway, just to gain leverage so I could stay over.

Shonda went on for hours without knowing that I couldn't care less.

Eventually I went to sleep, I can't remember if she was talking or not when I fell asleep.

I woke up to a door slamming, I jumped up and I focused my attention on the bedroom door, my vision was blurred, but I was still able to see an image by the door. It was a man that stood about 6 '2" and he had very dark skin and I began to panic.

This man just stood there in the door way and stared and I tried to wake up Shonda, I shoved on her and she turned around from her sleep and said close my damn door for I tell momma and he said with a loud raspy voice your momma said bring your ass here. Shonda said stop lying and he said she said now so when she come in here she gonna beat your ass and he slammed the door.

I immediately asked her when he left, who is that? She said that's my older brother and I asked her what time it was and she said it was 2:24 a.m.

Wow I must have been tired and I asked her what time did I go to sleep and she said girl you went to sleep at about 10:45 p.m. I thought to myself she must have bored the hell out me for me to go to sleep that early.

"Girl I think you need to go and see what your mother want," I said. She replied, "He better not be lying."

She got up and walked towards the door but before she could get to the door her mother busted through and said," I know damn well Velle told you I said come here."

Shonda replied "I was coming I was sleep, shoooooot."

Shonda walked out the room with her mom and she was gone for a while, but while she was gone I tried to get back in the comfortable spot I was in to go back to sleep, for some reason I couldn't relax.

The door opened again and there was her brother looking at me like a starved wolf.

I told him that Shonda went to talk to her mom and he said I knew. My next reply in my head was then what the hell do you want, but I was in complete silence, then I felt my heart racing and the anxiety approach within seconds.

"How old are you."

"17."

"What are you doing over here with Shonda this time of night?"

"I fell asleep and it's too late for me to be walking to my house."

"Your ass is lying. You ain't no damn 17 'cause Shonda ain't shit but 15, so how the hell are 17?"

In the back of my mind I became confused and overwhelmed at the same time and blurted out, "I ain't got to lie."

He said, "Well, if you are 17 you look young as hell. Stand up."

I was getting worried, wondering why he would want me to stand up. I stood up thinking in my mind, oh no not again.

He blurted out, "You sexy as hell girl!"

That made me feel uncomfortable and my stomach begin to feel sick.

He said, "My name is Velle and I am 24"

"Oh."

He asked, "What's up with me and you?"

"You are too old for me."

"When will you be 18?"

"Next year."

What month?"

I tried to make a joke saying, "Damn who are you the F.B.I?

He smiled and said, "You are funny as hell."

Just in the nick of time Shonda stormed through her room door and told Velle to get out and he said don't you see I'm talking to your friend and I was so relieved when she pushed his ass out the door and began to tell me not to listen to his pervert ass.

Little did she know that he was not on my agenda anyway? Shonda flopped on her bed and said that her mom was tripping because I was there, but she said I could stay until the morning and in my head I was like what the hell was her mom tripping for it's not like I was bothering her.

Morning approached and I must say I had a good night sleep. But the flies was irritating the hell out of me, I believe that's what woke me up. I felt so nasty and dirty I really needed a bath, but it was no way in hell I was taking a bath in that house considering the smell was terrible.

I had a sudden urge to go to the bathroom and I really didn't want to go because if the house smelled like piss I could just imagine how the bathroom smelled or even worse how it looked.

As I debated with my bladder, it seemed that my bladder won, so there I was making my way to the bathroom. I didn't have a clue where it was, but I wasn't going to wake Shonda up to find out because I probably would have shit on myself.

I made my way to the door, opened it, the screeching sound of the door scared the hell out of me. I looked both ways before I exited, the coast was clear. I saw a few doors and it wasn't hard for me to determine which door was the bathroom door because I heard water running.

I noticed that the light was on in the bathroom and that was a good thing because I didn't want to touch nothing trying to look for the light. The door was half opened it and walked in and almost fell out, it was roaches and flies everywhere and the toilet looked like it didn't work because of all the shit and toilet tissue that was in there. I gagged for a brief second. The toilet seat was cracked and somehow my urge to use the bathroom went away. I began to just wonder how in the hell can anyone even go in there to look in the mirror let alone use the bathroom.

I walked out backwards as if I had eyes in the back of my head and went back to Shonda's room in complete disgust. But I could even get in the room good her mom was walking towards the bathroom and said "good morning" and I said "good morning" and she walked in that bathroom with no problem and closed the door.

Yuk! Is all I could say in my head as she closed the bathroom door.

I finally got in the room and looked around, and I really felt sorry for Shonda because she didn't ask for the filth she was living in at least she kept her room kind of clean.

I snapped back to reality and remembered that I had to be on my way. I had to go to the bathroom and I was hungry, so I woke Shonda, told her thanks and told her I was about to leave.

"Why?"

I replied, "I have something to do."

"Okay" and she also told me to come back if I want.

In my head I was thinking, no time soon.

As I walked out the door, my thoughts began to wander and I had to call on my unseen friend to assist me in my thoughts. I just wanted to know what Shonda's thoughts were, I wanted to know was the norm that she was living in her mind. Can love blind us of the things that we know that are wrong? Well even after talking to my unseen friend I had no answer.

So my journey continues.

5

After walking for a long period of time that sudden urge to go to the toilet came back, so I had to find somewhere to use the bathroom. I knew I couldn't cop a squat in the alley because I didn't have any tissue and I couldn't take a chance on getting caught in action.

I saw a Mickey D's, so I began to walk towards it and as I walked down the street I saw a yard with some cloths on a clothing line, you know the ropes that be tied to the poles so you could hang your clothing on them to dry.

Yes! I went and grabbed me some clean clothes off of the clothing line and some gym shoes. Boy! I tell you I hit the jackpot that day. I felt so bad but it felt so right at the time.

However, I still realized that I had to use the bathroom, but I still managed to hold it. I went to a friend's house around my house because at the time it seemed to be a good idea.

I ended up at my friend Tasha's house and she was pretty cool about letting me in and I had nowhere to go so I had to appreciate what I could get at the time. Tasha's house was not all that nice or clean, but it was good enough to rest.

When I walked in, I smelled fried chicken and considering I was famished at that point I really didn't give a damn how her house looked. Her mother was in the kitchen cooking and had on some dirty clothing, but that hunger pain that was in my stomach was impulsive and that's when that magical moment came, she offered me some chicken and I didn't even let her finish all of the sentence before I abruptly answered and said yes ma'am.

Yes, I did use the word "ma'am", because I learned that responding in a respectful matter gained favor to the old folks. I sat down in the kitchen and waited patiently for the food that she was about to give me and I noticed a roach crawling up the wall, I tried to ignore it, but the walls were white and the roach looked like a black spot moving and every so often I would glance over to find out the roach location because I didn't want to eat it.

However, the roach was a distraction, but the chair that I was sitting in was poking me and I hurt and all I could do is try to adjust my butt in the seat. Finally, she gave my plate and I scanned the kitchen to locate the roach and there it was right on the ceiling right over me like a dam mistletoe, I didn't want to jeopardize my food, so I casually stood up and away from the roach.

I really felt as if the roach was antagonizing me, almost like it knew what it was doing. I ate my food and soon afterwards I just felt sick to my stomach just thinking about what had happen to earlier with the rape and all. I went to the bathroom to throw up and it was so nasty in there was almost like it assisted me in throwing up.

I felt at that moment taking a bath wasn't an option because the rust and the dirt ring was having an argument and I just wanted to find a spot to just go get some sleep.

I found a slot on the couch and it was okay, but I just couldn't sleep because of the rape, I was so scared and I cried when I just knew everyone was sleep. I cried all that night to myself and talking to someone inside my head, I don't have a clue to whom I was talking to in my head, but somehow it was comforting.

The morning was approaching, I could feel the sun beaming on my cheekbone. I knew from the amount of light that was outside it was pretty early and the birds were chirping which was very annoying.

I got up and stretched my body, I was still sore, so I kind of lost my balance and fell backward on the couch. I got back up and noticed that no one was woke, so I walked over to the kitchen and peeped in the refrigerator and it was no surprise that it wasn't a lot of food in there, it was mostly spoiled food and filth that filled the refrigerator.

I walked towards the door and opened it, I felt like I was a vampire, the sun was beaming so hard. I walked on the porch and I was on my way to my next pit stop, which only God knew where that was.

I began walking and my thoughts were rotating around in my head, as if I was some type of robot with a short circuit. As I was walking I somehow came to the neighborhood playground and found myself drawn to the swing and I walked towards the swing, looked up at the poles because I wanted to make sure that the swing was secure.

Living in the ghetto was risky on a daily basis because everything was either broken or just didn't work. I took a seat on the swing and slowly swung, thinking, and tears began to fill my eyes but for some reason these tears were different, they were strong like once they rolled down my face they felt as if they were burning my face. I can't even began to pinpoint why I was crying because they were so many reasons but I knew my heart was aching which lead to my tears.

After crying for about ten minutes or so I then began to hear that familiar voice of my unseen friend. All I could hear was *it will be okay, I will take care of you and protect you.* At that point I felt a sense of comfort.

Deep down I just wanted to go home but I could not take a chance on going back and getting beat. Sometimes I would daydream my mother crying and looking for me. I would also picture her finding me and running towards me hugging me and saying how much she missed me and apologizing to me for hurting me.

Reality kicked in and interrupted my Little House on the Prairie moment. Time seemed as if was moving fast before I knew it, it was three hours later and I stood up from the swing, wiped my face with my sleeves and began walking towards the playground exit.

Before I could focus my eye sight right, the police were parked in front of the playground. I began to panic silently, my first instinct was to run like hell.

However, I walked toward the water fountain and I wanted to look behind me as I walked, but I just kept walking. I nervously leaned toward the fountain and I heard their police radios as if they were right behind me.

I believe I was drinking that water for about two minutes before I heard someone say, "Hey you."

I tried to focus on drinking the water, but I could feel someone behind me and the police radios sounds were close at this point. I knew the police were behind me.

I thought about running but I was briefly reminded by my feet that I was pigeon- toed, you know, that's when your feet are pointed toward each other. I knew I would trip over my own feet if I tried to run.

I tried to ignore them as if I didn't know they were talking to me. My stomach began to do flips and that weird feeling hit me like I'm caught! In those few moments I had a million different thoughts going on in my head. I finally relaxed my face and turned around and looked at them and asked, "You're talking to me?

They police said, "Yes, come here let us talk to you for a second."

I walked towards them and said, "Huh?"

They asked me my name and I quickly said, "Tasha Parks."

They asked me where I lived.

I said, "Spaulding and Wabansia."

They then asked me for the address and that's when it all fell apart because I didn't have a clue what my fried address was, so I paused and said any address.

These guys looked at me and then they looked at each other. I knew at that point my journey was over. They asked me how old was I so I said 17 and the police asked me for my I.D and I told them I forgot it at home.

It was a Hispanic officer and an African American officer. The Hispanic officer had a piece of paper in his hands. He leaned over and whispered to the African-American officer, I don't know what he was saying but I'm sure that it wasn't good.

Then the Hispanic officer said, "Young lady, there is no reason to keep this charade going on, we know that you are a runaway and your name is Lunye Williams."

At that moment, it seemed as if everything in the world stood still and silence filled the air. I didn't know what to say, all I knew is my stomach felt as if it fell out of my ass. The Black officer asked me if I had any sharp objects on me and I said no.

He asked me to turn around and put my hands behind me, but that urge of running ran across my mind and I knew that it would be a waste of time so I cooperated and that's when the Hispanic officer cuffed me.

6

The officers walked me towards the police car and I began to cry as if I was going to the electric chair. They helped me into the car and I kept telling them the cuffs was too tight and they ignored me.

As I sat in the back seat watching the officers walk to their seats I began to allow my mind to rapidly move into the future, seeing my mother and it wasn't a pretty vision. I began to mentally yell for my unseen friend and he was nowhere to be found.

Finally the officers got in the car and slammed the car doors which made me jump because I was just plain old scared. Before I knew it, I began to start begging and pleading for my freedom. The officers were not trying to hear my heart felt pleas to be released.

The Black officer asked me why did I runaway? And I told him that it wasn't part of my plan but my mother locked me out.

The officer told me that I was lying and all I wanted to do is hang out with the gang bangers and he also stated that my mother's boyfriend was a good friend of his, Officer Henry.

My mouth dropped and my stomach begin to do flips because at this point I knew I wasn't going to win. It was a bumpy and a very uncomfortable ride.

My arm began to feel as if it was going to dislocate, so I took it upon myself to release myself from the cuffs on my own. I watched the police as I dislocated my thumbs this is something that I did and I didn't know I could until I was about ten years old. I then slid my hands out of the cuffs and it seemed so easy, I just made sure I kept my hands behind my back to keep the officers from pulling over and putting them back on.

The ride seemed so long but that gave me a little time to think. Before I knew it the Hispanic police threw that piece of paper that he was holding at me. I wanted to grab it but I remembered that I had slipped my hands out the cuffs and they did not know it and I did not want to give myself away.

So, I asked curiously, "What is that?"

The Black officer said "Your missing report, you are famous Miss Lady."

I couldn't say much of nothing and I continued thinking of a master plan.

We finally made it to the police station and it almost felt as if we were going into a bat cave or something. When the officers parked the car, I then remembered that I did not have on my handcuffs and this may become a problem once they figured it out, so I dislocated my thumbs and slid the handcuffs on before they could open the back door of the police car.

They pulled me out and began to tease me about going to the big house a.k.a jail. I was really scared at this point and I could feel the tear well up in my eyes.

The Black officer said "It's too late to cry now."

I wanted to tell him to shut the hell up so bad but due to the power these guys had over me I held my peace and it wasn't like I had the juice or nothing, it was just creating a tough thought in my mind.

Once I actually entered the police station, the smell drove me nuts. All I could hear were phones ringing, loud chatter and typing on the typewriters. The police handled me as if I was a hard core criminal holding me by my cuffs and leading me to a processing interview room.

Once I entered the room, I began to panic silently, the room they took me too looked exactly like those rooms on T.V. It was two desks, each one had a typewriter on it and a lot of papers.

I then really started panicking when I saw a long metal like bench with multiple metal looking rings embedded into a brick wall that covered the room. They told me to have a seat and they walked me over to the bench and unhooked one of my cuffs which brought me some comfort.

The Hispanic officer then connected that loose cuff to the metal ring on the brick wall. The Black officer took a seat at one the desks and the Hispanic officer left the room. This made me feel weird for some reason, time flew by and the Black officer was typing and I didn't have a clue about what but the noise was annoying me.

Finally the Hispanic officer came back in and I asked a question "Why am still here?"

The Hispanic officer said "We are waiting on your parents to get here."

I said "Parents?"

He said, "Yes."

I told him I had only one active parent, so they must be making a mistake.

I already knew who he was talking about, Henry, the so-called police officer. I did not want to see his face at all. The thought of seeing him made my stomach sick. I just wanted to start telling everything but I was so scared, I just started to cry. The tears wear so potent they made my face burn. I felt like I was in jail without being in jail. I was just hoping and praying that they would just send me to jail, because I believe being in jail would be that more safe for me.

As the thoughts and anxious feelings took control of me, I began to sweat because I felt the demons coming closer in my spirit. It was almost like someone was warning me they were coming.

I contacted my unseen friend, he took a bit of time to come but eventually he tuned in and I informed him of my trouble and it was like he knew already, I thought this was very weird but hey, I had more important things to figure out.

My unseen friend told me to wipe my tears and hold my head up, so I did just that. Listening to his encouraging words had me feeling invincible, almost like I could rule the whole world. The reality kicked in when I heard the police say you guys can step right this way.

My stomach didn't flip, it turned around and tried to escape my body. I tried to turn my head and look at the bricks on the wall. I even attempted to count them.

I heard Henry say, "Ne-Ne, why would you do this to your mother?"

At that moment my thoughts took me back to the Hulk and I wish that I could turn to that big ugly monster at this time, but my thoughts were interrupted by a touch on the shoulders.

"Don't you hear me talking to you?"

I then turned around without giving either one of them eye contact and said "I don't know" so then it was a moment of silence. I then felt my arm pit starting to drench with water, well realistically speaking sweat.

I casually looked over at my mother and it almost looked like her eyes were red like she was crying, so this gave me hope I thought this may have created some type of change or something. I began to feel at peace for the moment.

Now this was big for me because the only time I have seen this lady cry was after a good ass whipping from my father. So, my mom and I finally made eye contact and the teary eyes did not match the look in her eyes.

Something wasn't right and it made me feel uneasy. The police and my parents must have walked away during the time I was engaging in my multiple thoughts because I didn't see them, it's almost like they vanished and I was right there, which would have been a good idea at the time, well at least for me. I tried to make contact with my unseen friend because I was getting very scared and he didn't tune in and this is not like him at all. He always there when I'm scared.

Now I am worried because my unseen friend abandoned me at the worst time of my life at that moment. Just like any other the time, they walked in and interrupted my thoughts and told me to come on.

I almost acted as if they were not talking to me.

Henry said, "Didn't you hear me? Let's go." He said, with a voice that made me feel like the day when he told me to take off my clothes in that attic before he beat me.

And just as before my mother stood there as if she didn't give a damn. Now her actions made me feel as if she was crying because that was what parents supposed to do if their children were missing. I finally got up and I was moving so slow I made a turtle look like a rabbit because I just didn't want to go home.

I finally got close enough to them and my mother said her first words to me.

"You might as bring your mother fucking ass on here." It was almost alike a death sentence, because those were her exact words.

Now this was become a serious concern, I had a different vision after seeing her eyes watery. My vision was her hugging and saying, do this shit no more, now you know it would have been B.S. if I didn't add a curse word.

Well back to my mirage of her hugging me close to her busom and this magical music playing in the background. I think I am going to go over board and have her to spin me around and say I love you. Not to mention some fairy dust and glitter falling from the sky creating a magical scene that made this mythical magical moment even better.

Again my daydream was interrupted by my mother telling me to get in the car. I got in the car and this overwhelming feeling came over me as if I was getting in the car with two demons.

They got in the car, the doors slammed and it sounded like cell block one shutting down. My heart began to race and my palms began to sweat. After hearing complete silence after they pulled off, I had to go the bathroom. I have no idea why I had to use the bathroom because I didn't eat nothing. I just tried to stay positive and think the best out of a bad situation.

We finally pulled up to the house and I thought to myself maybe I should tell them what happened to me while being on the streets, but that was like telling the devil that someone raped me. It was so quiet that the silence was loud. My heart was racing a million miles per hour and I had that bubble gut moment as we got out the car. I wanted to run, but my legs were not cooperating at the time. I knew that they were not too happy with me by the way they slammed the car doors.

We walked towards our apartment and I walked very slowly behind them.

My mother yelled out, "Bring your ass on here for I help you out."

Then my legs all of a sudden start to work because they began to move fast.

Henry went up the stairs, my mother stayed behind I guess to make sure I got in and to make sure that door was locked. As I got closer to the door I was focused on how I was going to get pass her without taking a fist to the face.

I felt that way because she always made it her business to knock the hell out of us when we walked pass her, only if we did something that was wrong. I got closer and closer and I made it to the door where she was standing there looking like an evil person.

I walked pass her and ducked and walked at the same time. I was shocked. I ran up those stairs so fast you would have thought I was running a marathon. I made it upstairs and I could hear her feet stomping up the stairs, the closer she got the more I got scared.

By the time my mom got up the stairs, I had fled to my room and I heard her slam the door and I was praying that she didn't call me or come to my room. God must have heard my prayers because she went to her room with Henry. I heard them talking, I was so scared I didn't even want to ease drop.

My sisters and my brother were in the room in complete silence and the look in their eyes looked more like I feel sorry for you and then my thought process was interrupted by my mother's room door opening and I heard her walking towards my room calling my name.

I knew it was too good to be true for her to go to bed and leave me the hell alone.

I replied "Yes!"

This how we had to reply to her and it was fine to me, but she would talk to us any kind of way. I thought you are supposed to lead by example, I guess that's an understatement.

After I replied, she said, "I don't know what the fuck you think this is but you better get your ass in there and take a motherfucking bath."

I replied, "Okay", but in the back of my mind I was like how does one person say so many curse words in one sentence. I did what she asked and got my night clothing and took a bath and of course I made sure I cleaned up behind myself.

When I got out of the bathroom from getting my hygiene together, I walked back to the room. My siblings were just looking at me like I was a monster or something.

I asked them, "What are you looking at?"

They didn't say anything so this told me my mother told them not to talk to me that was cool because I didn't feel like talking anyway.

I threw my dirty clothing in the hamper and climbed in the bed and began to silently calling my unseen friend and he never appeared.

I grabbed pen, paper and began to write. I wrote about my thoughts and feelings at the time and they were not nice at all. The day went by really fast, before you knew it, it was night. I fell asleep writing. I woke up at about three o'clock in the morning because I had a nightmare of my mother and Henry killing me and I was just running. I so glad I woke up before they caught me.

I was also really happy I woke up because my writings were in eyesight where my mother could see them. I folded them up really small and hid them at the bottom of our dresser. I was very tired and the bed felt great, but I was still feeling a little funny so I closed the room door so Henry wouldn't get a sudden urge to come talk to me.

I laid back down and I began to cry out of the blue. I just felt like I didn't belong, I didn't want to be there. I finally cried myself back to sleep and I was awaken by pots and pans slamming together.

I got out my bed and I believe it was about 7a.m., and I was still tired. But my mother screamed mine and my siblings name to come and eat. It was the typical oatmeal breakfast.

We washed up and ate our breakfast and it was so strange that my siblings still didn't say a word to me. We did the normal routine; eat, wash dishes and go back to the room. Something was different today because she told me to put on my clothes and didn't tell my siblings, now this was weird. I finally got all dressed up.

Henry came out the room and walked to the front door and my mother followed and my mother blurted out for me to "bring your ass on here". I followed even though I was scared.

We got in the car and they pulled off. I had so many bad thoughts. I noticed we pulled up in front of this hospital called St. Anne's hospital and they told me to get out. I didn't have a clue to what was going on. We got on the elevator and went to the fourth floor and I figured it out when I saw mental health. They are going to put me in a nut house.

Oh no!

7

My shock caused me to become short of breath. I immediately felt tears welling up, I tried to hold them back but there was no control and a tear came out of my right eye so fast, I wiped it off before anyone could see it.

We approached the main desk, I don't know what was said because I blocked out all sound and became isolated in my own body. I remember following them to some seats sat down. I almost felt death at the time.

My palms became sweaty and it was almost painful to hold back my tears. The room was spinning momentarily and I had to hold on to the arm rest of my seat. I begin to call on my unseen friend because I didn't understand what was going on or why. My unseen friend never answered and this made it hard to hold back my tears.

Tears invaded my face like a waterfall. I wiped them away as fast as they were coming down. I began to observe my surroundings and I saw a few kids my age walking past and there was one in particular that caught my attention. I saw a guy that was dressed like a girl and this was very confusing to me. My thoughts were interrupted by a white lady coming out and greeting my mother and Henry.

The lady looked very pleasant, she had a smile on her face that lit up the room, but somehow I knew she was up to no good. The lady asked us to follow her to a room and I noticed as I was walking that the boy that was dressed like a girl walked past us and he waived at me.

I was still baffled by the way he was dressed because he was a boy. He had on some skin tight stonewashed jeans and he had on what looked like a body shirt and it was quite tight, he also had on some make-up and pumps. His hair was like neck length and kind of messy.

Even though he had on girl clothing it was quite obvious that he was a boy because of his bone structure and not to mention the bulge in front of his pants that clearly stated he had man parts.

We made it to the office and we were led to take a seat. We all took a seat and my mood changed very quickly, I was very angry and defensive, which may have not been a good idea at that time. The lady said hello to me and asked me how was feeling.

I looked over at my mother and Henry and just decided not to say anything at all. For one I was scared because these evil people that brought me in that hospital had full control and who knows what they would do next.

My attention was then drawn back towards the lady, she asked me why did I runaway. I wanted to just blurt out everything and but I was a nobody; who would believe me over my mother and a cop. I just sat in silence and refused to answer.

Then she blurted out "Your mother tells me that you like to make up stories and say things that are not true."

I became very angry after this I looked at them both with so much hate and before you know it my mouth had a mind of its own and I said, "I don't be lying!"

The lady said, "Well tell me, what is the problem at home?"

I then said "They be messing with me."

And the lady asked who?

I pointed at my mother and Henry without looking at them because looking at them would only scare me.

I began to cry because I was scared and just thinking about the things that I went through was very hurtful for me.

My mother tried to say something but the lady interrupted her and told her to please let me speak and my mother then said she ain't go do nothing but lie. After my mother opened her mouth I shut down.

The lady then asked me, "How would you feel if you spent a few days here so we can help you deal with your problems without running away?"

Well at that point in time it sounded like a really good idea because the way they were looking at me there is no telling what they would have done with me once we left.

So, I am thinking this was premeditated, no papers were signed or nothing.

The lady told me to say my goodbye's because I would be there thirty days.

My eyes then opened very wide and I was not expecting to stay that long, but hey anything to get away from them.

Henry's phony ass asked me if I needed anything and I just said no. My mother couldn't even fake she game a damn about me.

The lady left to get me ready for intake so that meant I had to be alone with them demons.

My mother first words were, "You better get your shit together or you gone be your ass in here a long time."

I looked at her with disbelief and had a head conversation with her, meaning I spoke only in my mind. *I would think if you have not seen your child in weeks and then you are turning her over to a behavioral center, you may just want to drop those three words "I love you".*

Maybe I am living in a fairytale land.

After the so called goodbyes, the nice lady came back in and told me to follow her. I walked behind her and took one last look at my mother and hoped she would just change her mind and just have a sudden change of heart and just blurt out *Lunye' I love you and I want you to come home* and she would tell Henry to get the hell out of our lives.

Unfortunately, it was only a mirage, but one that would make my breath worth breathing. My mirage disappeared when the nice lady asked me to follow her.

My heart felt like it had stopped beating for a moment, tears begin to invade my face and they were uncontrollable. I tried wiping them away but they were coming as fast as I was wiping them.

The nice lady told me it will be okay and they were going to help me do what I have to do to go home to my mom.

The lady walked me to a room and she told me that I had to remove all my property from my pockets, what she didn't know is I didn't have much; but a dollar and some change.

Anyhow, I emptied my pockets and every other second I wiped away my tears. The lady then told me that I would have to shower and she asked me if I had a change of clothing and I looked at her as if she asked a stupid question because I didn't have a bag.

I responded with a sarcastic *no* and she said they have clothing that is donated to the hospital that I could wear, so don't worry. I then began to wonder why my mom didn't give me clothing to take with me.

This thought made me recall a moment when my mom told me I don't own shit in her house; she told me that I was just renting everything. Well this has pretty much given me my answer.

The lady led me to the shower room and for some reason I felt safe but disoriented at the same time. I walked into the shower room and it was so spacy.

I turned on the shower and out of the blue my unseen friend said, how are you?

He scared me for a second, but I was so happy to talk to him it really didn't matter. I pretty much just filled him in on what happened and let him know that I was upset that he did not answer when I called.

He told me if I really wanted to talk to him I would have got him. So, I didn't understand what that meant so I left that conversation alone. I began to scrub my body and continue my conversation.

Even though I was naked, I didn't feel weird when my unseen friend was around and from my knowledge he was a man, well at least he sounded like one.

I heard a knock at the shower door and I knew that meant they wanted me to come out. I had to tell my unseen friend that I had to go and I would talk to him later.

I opened the door with nothing but a towel around me and I just stood there, of course, waiting on the lady to give me clothes, instead she gave me a hospital gown and in my head I remembered her saying they would give me clothing. I put on the gown and she lead me to the laundry center, I guess I spoke to soon be she showed me bins of clothing and told me to pick what I liked.

I took my time, as if I was at Macy's. I finally found some cute clothing, I noticed that they were used but I didn't care, it was better than what I had on coming in. Once I got my clothing on, I was led into what they called the family room where there were a lot of kids about my age there.

Everybody was looking at me, in fact they were staring so hard I believed they were able to see through my clothing.

They were having a group meeting and they were talking about feelings I guess. I really did care for that too much. I was asked to introduce myself, I told them my name and left it at that, but the group counselor asked me why was I there and I blurted out, ***for nothing***.

Then I got an audience. I heard chatter saying, *me too I didn't even do nothing, my mother hates me and she don't like me.* In so many ways I was able to relate to those kids.

The counselor asked us all to settle down and it was time to close the meeting, we all held hands and said some encouraging poem and we went to our rooms.

I didn't have a clue to where my room was until I asked one of the staff and they said 22A, I walked to my room and to my surprise it was really nice and neat. I walked into the room and I was so happy I was thinking at this moment I could live there forever.

It had a nice twin bed, a desk with a lamp, and I also noticed there was a dresser. The desk interested me the most because I would be able to write and writing is something I missed.

My thoughts became more positive after seeing my room even though I had to share a room with someone else.

I flopped on the bed and I fell asleep.

Before I knew it was dinner time and we were to all report to the lunch room area. I pretty much kind of followed others to the lunch room that was how I found my way around. I got in line and behind me I felt a tap on my shoulder and I turned around and it was that guy that I had seen, you know the one that was dressed a like a girl.

He gave me a hug and said his name was Frank but everybody calls him Fefe and I told him my name. We hit it off pretty good, he was really friendly and so was I. We ate our dinner together and just talked and talked.

Dinner was finally over and we had to go to our rooms and get ourselves prepared for bed because we had school the next day. I went to my room and I kicked my feet up and thought to myself I could stay here forever.

I never thought I would want to stay in a damn nut house, but it was pretty cool friends, meals and a roof over your head. Before you knew it was the next morning and it was time to get ready for school and I got myself dressed with what I had on yesterday. I was clean that's all that mattered.

We all lined up and we were taken to school and I was quite nervous but hey you had to follow rules.

School was pretty nice and I must say easy, well easy for me. I was getting kind of bored, but I did stay engaged with what the teacher was teaching.

We only stayed in class for about a couple of hours and we were off again to the family room.

Everything seemed so systematic there, but it worked for me and it kept me busy. Writing really became my friend in this hospital because the peace allowed me to get involved with being expressive with my thoughts.

It seemed as if time flew by in the hospital because my friends were leaving and new people were coming in and the only one I had left is Frank, and we had become so close we used to call each other sisters. He would tell me the things that he went through and why he became gay and I would cry and just hug him, I told him my story and he cried and hugged me as well.

It was something about Frank I couldn't shake it, he was just a beautiful person and he always had a smile on his face.

It was about that time for me to leave and I was in disbelief that thirty days had gone so fast!

I began to ask the staff if I could just stay a little while longer and they said no that I had to go home.

Here we go again, the tears begin to flow and I just wanted to scream. I know my mother did not change because she didn't come to visit me one time throughout my thirty day stay. I just didn't want to go back, I didn't know what to do, my friend Frank told me that if I did something crazy that they would send me back and I didn't want to do that because that would make her lies become true.

I just went to my room and packed all my things that I accumulated throughout the time I was there. It was 6 p.m. and surprisingly they were on time to pick me up.

When I saw them, I put my head down because I didn't want to look them in their face, but surprisingly my mother hugged me and this was not normal and they had bags.

Henry walked up and asked me how do I felt? I was so shocked I couldn't say nothing at all. I thought this was some kind of joke. It was time to go and the shock distracted me on my thoughts and feelings of leaving my new friends.

I just followed them to the elevator and I begin to rub my eyes to see if it was a dream. We all stood by the elevator in pretty much in silence. I was very nervous and my palms became very sweaty. I began to tap on the walls of the elevator and suddenly I heard a ding and the doors opened.

I followed my mother and Henry out of the elevator and I was feeling kind of weird like any moment they were going to start cursing and beating on me, but they didn't.

As I followed them to the car I felt anxious and very unsettled but I had to keep my composure so I would upset them. I got in the car and they pulled off and I felt like I was leaving with the devil or something.

The drive was a smooth one.

Henry blurted out "What did you learn up in the hospital?"

I hesitated momentarily and said, "Umm, umm, umm, to be good at home and to respect your parents." Even though in the back of my mind I felt as if they should have been the one locked up.

Henry then replied back "You know we are really proud of you".

And then he said, "Aint we momma?" Shoving on my mother. She looked and him and rolled her eyes and told him to not be bumping on her. I knew at that point it was all some B.S., I knew it was too good to be true, the look on her face told it all.

We finally pulled up to the house and I went to open the door and my mother said, "Make sure you get your ass up there and clean that closet in y'all's room. I was okay with that just as long as she didn't hit me.

We made it up the stairs and I noticed that the kids were not there and this puzzled me but I wouldn't dare to ask because that was like asking a lion for some of his food, it would snap on you. I just did what she asked and cleaned the room, I even organized it like I was a professional.

Once I cleaned the room, I grabbed my made up diary and began to write, after about thirty minutes I called my unseen friend to keep him updated.

Just as I thought he didn't appear, this made me so mad, it seemed like every time I want to talk my friend, he was never available.

I knew it was too good to be true, my mother called me and I mean she scared the hell up out of me.

I then said loudly, "Here I come."

I finally found her standing in the kitchen staring at the refrigerator. It was not food so I don't know why she was just standing there like she was in a trance.

She blurted out, "Clean this kitchen and clean behind the stove."

I really wanted to tell her to kiss my ass, so I just did what I was told. It took a while but I got it done, I went back to my room because my unseen friend popped up outta nowhere. I had to make way to my room before he left because I couldn't talk to him in front of anyone they would have thought I was crazy like you guys are thinking now.

I made it to the room and I filled my friend in on everything and what concerned me the most is they were kind of being nice. My unseen friend told me to be watchful because they were trying to trick me.

I then went back to writing and eventually I got tired and went to sleep without anything to eat. Before you know it, it was morning time went by so fast but, hey, I really wish it would go express so I could be 18 to get the hell out of my mother's house.

My days were pretty much the same for about a week until my siblings came back home. Of course my brother was always the cool one but those two little sisters of mines, I thought they were the devil spawns.

Well my siblings were home and the house was quiet and they started taking toys out and pretty much messing up the room I took my time to clean. I took the toys from them and put them back up and Desire hit me and bit me afterwards, now, I am not going to lie, my reflexes has a mind of its own.

I slapped her up side her head so hard she immediately started to scream.

Now meanwhile she done bit me and broke skin and made me bleed. My sister ran in my mom's room and told her I hit her.

My mom said, "Come here Lunye."

I pretended I didn't hear her, I was thinking maybe she was going to blow it off.

I was in for a rude awakening and the second time she called me she said "Bitch, I know you hear me calling your motherfucking ass."

I replied, "Yes"

She said, "Come here bitch."

I said, "Mama she bit me and hit me first, I was trying to keep the room clean."

My mom told me that I was getting my ass whipped for putting my hands on Desire. Now, in my mind this sounded like some bogus B.S.

Before I knew it, she jumped up and got to punching me. I felt my lip split and I could feel the warm blood leaking, you would think that would make her stop hell naw it seemed like that made her beat me more.

I was thinking the whole time she was beating me that I was going to call somebody on her ass. I was in a lot of pain and I think I was more hurt from the words that were coming out of her mouth.

After she got tired beating me, she was coughing, as if she was having a hard time breathing. Can you believe that I was still concerned about her?

I had knots everywhere and my face was pretty bruised. I couldn't take this no more, I had to wait till it got dark and I had to make sure they were sleep to leave.

I waited until the sun went down to make my move. I had plans on never coming back home. I was very sore and emotional at this time.

Most of all, I was scared and I was very angry at my mother. After writing and getting my a few clothes together, it was time for me to make my move. I grabbed my things and fled out the back door. I looked back several times just to make sure that I wanted to leave and I was more than sure. Here I go again back out on the streets.

There I was on my new journey, I wasn't walking no more than 30 minutes before I was approached by a guy who rode up on me and said, "You shouldn't be out here by yourself."

I said, "I am grown."

He said, "Okay. Let me take you to where you need to go."

I said, "I don't know you."

He said, "I will show you my id to prove who am."

He pulled out the id and I don't have a clue to why I took a chance on trusting this man but I got in the car.

He said, "You should not get into cars with men you don't know because it's dangerous."

He smiled and turned down a dark alley and I began to have that scary feeling once and again....

What did I get myself into this time...?

Deception

Deception has created strife and hate in our communities and allowed evil to take part in our hearts.

We have allowed suppressed feelings to resurface the atmosphere assisting the devil with devour souls and rip our lives apart.

Every day blood sheds, every day hearts break, however we neglect the good book that will take all the pain away

Broken hearts are awakened from passed hurt, harm and danger, now evil has awaken seeking revenge causing hurt and harm to total strangers.

Tales from the dark side have become our bright side, giving the enemy ammunition to take control of our bruised minds.

The illusions of the murderous trends has distracted the message that Lord has given us within.

The devil has taken flight and taken over the once beautiful world that we live in.

Love has come to a minimum and disrespect is our new high.

Why won't we listen, how many of our people have to continue to die?

Painful memories have taken over our true inner being, reluctant to bring forth peace living in rage enjoying the hell we live in.

Is it because of the pain from way back then, the pain I suppressed when I was a kid?

Never an apology which caused me to live my abuse over and over again.

Ignoring the truth each time a child is abused, instead of speaking up we become accessories after the fact to this word called ABUSE!

My message to you is: Speak up when you see a child being abused because if you don't it will create a domino effect of bad decisions and later fill the world with hate and worst of all self-hate.

By Danette King

LET'S SPEAK ON IT

Healing

We've all been through an amount of stressful situations in life, however, some more traumatic than others: Abuse, to be more precise, mental, physical, sexual, and drug abuse. These issues require patience and persistence. Like most I'm not an advocate of the "get over it, it's the past" cliché, or any other for that matter. I find them to be disrespectful. Things we go through in life that create trauma, which requires a healing process: If you fall and a scar appears, the scar does not just disappear, it takes time for a scar to heal and not only that, it can leave a permanent mark behind, depending on the severity of the scar. We spend most of our lives suppressing unresolved issues to only one day find out that they really don't disappear. Needless to say your scar have become a part of you and it's up to you to incorporate it as a part of who you have become, accept it never be ashamed of it. I don't have medical credentials only theories, logics and cold hard experience. Now it's time to face your pain and evict it out of your heart and your head because it may just be over crowded. When the pain leave that when the healing process begins, but remember there will always be a scar left behind. Let's try writing all of your most detrimental issues on paper and after each one write your feelings towards each situation until you get tired, this could take days or even months it depends on you... Some might not enjoy writing, this is optional: like singing, rapping, talking, even though art. This technique is very flexible and you are able to customize it your lifestyle. Once you have expounded on your issues write them on a piece of paper and get a glass of water and dropped the paper in the glass and sit and watch it dissolve. How did that make you feel? Email me and let's speak on it
"Subtract suppression and add progression."

Aftermath

We spoke briefly about dealing and coping with suppressed issues. We talked about a healing process that can be tailored to fit your lifestyle. Now let's expound on the aftermath of how your emotional state of mind is. Today we are going to talk about how to move forward from these situation without looking back.

Rule 1. Love yourself. Go in the mirror and ask yourself, do I love you? This is a question that makes you examine yourself and questions the behaviors towards oneself. Asking yourself questions like "How do I love myself" do you plant love into your mind body soul? When you plant seeds in a garden, you do what is necessary to insure that the plant grows successful. If you don't tend to your garden, it doesn't flourish properly, and even worse it can die. Treat yourself like that beautiful garden, take time to self because no one can take care of your garden like you can. You and only you know how you want that garden to look and what is necessary to insure it's the best garden that anyone has ever seen. No one else should benefit from the fruits of your labor, and no one else is going to tend to your garden like you can, and way too often we let people into that area for the end results to be weeds, pests, and even snakes if we're not too careful. Plant the seeds that are needed so you can radiate beauty and health within your mind body and soul.

Rule 2. Reprogram the way you think. By reprogramming the way you think, you are focusing on recreating more positive thought patterns, instead of when you when go through a present stressful situation we are going to retrain our minds to revisit thoughts that were more positive in your life. For example, when you go shopping, do you go to the clothing rack to pick out the ugliest outfit in the store even when we feel ugly that day? Of course not. We go shopping to make us feel better, because when we look good we feel good. It's the same principal that you apply to reprogramming your mindset, you take things that feel better about your life and "wear "them with confidence.

Rule 3. Last but not least, say what you mean, and mean what you say. For example, thought processes can be very confusing and is to be taken very seriously. The first process is to develop the thought, the second process is to analyze, and the last process is to speak these thoughts into existence once we have come to some logical conclusion on whatever the thought was. Once it's in the speaking process which is the last part of the process, these words should then become action. The good part about this process is that you can edit it if you want, we are human and we make mistakes. However, do no neglect the thought, but make sure it is a positive thought. We do know the difference between positive and negative, of course negative meaning it could be detrimental, and positive thoughts meaning things that will secure your success. Let's say you are trying to lock in employment for a managerial position, but you don't have the proper credentials to qualify for the position. You began to break down and analyze the things that are necessary to achieve this goal. Sometimes we have to go back and edit our thoughts which in turn edits our overall actions, for instance, maybe you were going to school to secure this ideology, but life events happened to pull back. Never give up on the action to complete your first thought because nine times out of ten our first mind is always better than the second. Continue to analyze your thoughts because in turn it will help your execute your actions with more precision.

Let your journey be a compliment of your thoughts. Email me. Let's speak on it!

Establishing your foundation

We talked about how to retrain our thought process, which may have aroused questions as to what's next. Let's work on giving you a pat on your back for establishing your foundations.

Congratulate yourself for establishing your foundation is like graduating from eighth grade that was the first time you felt of importance and being excited about going to high school. Today is a day of celebration, you are now on the path of getting to know, and even better loving yourself. So our sole purpose is to treat ourselves for taking the initiative to establish our foundation. If you have not done this lately, treat yourself to a meal and engage in self conversation of how proud you are of yourself. These are one of the many things we need to do in life to be proud of ourselves, because no one else will do that but you. Treat yourself to those brand new pair of shoes or a piece of jewelry, these are like diplomas for accomplishments of the steps you have taken to loving yourself. Now you have a "diploma" that you can go back and look at when you are going through a difficult time in life. When you are upset, you can go home and put on those pairs of shoes and feel good, or you can go back and look at that piece of jewelry and realize you came a long way. Just like you save receipts, whatever you chose to do save that receipt and keep as your "Diploma" so you can revisit it in the event you have a "Pop Quiz" which can be negative thoughts invading your mind.

A foundation is a necessity in the principles of completion.

How do you feel? Send me a picture of your "diploma" if you like and I'll post them. Email me, lets speak on it.

NOTES

NOTES

NOTES

NOTES

Coming in 2016

Series 3

The Third Installment of Danette King's Exciting and Eye-opening Memoir.

Don't Miss It!

www.ingramcontent.com/pod-product-compliance
Lightning Source LLC
Chambersburg PA
CBHW031427290426
44110CB00011B/565